print making with a spoon

norman gorbaty

reinhold publishing corporation, new york

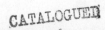

to my father

©1960, Reinhold Publishing Corporation
All rights reserved
Printed in the United States of America

Designed by Myron Hall III
Printed and type set by Comet Press
Bound by Russell-Rutter Company, Inc.

Library of Congress Catalog Card Number 60-9671

contents

acknowledgements

Alvin Eisenman, lecturer in the graphic arts at Yale University, for his aid and direction in the formulation of "Printmaking with a Spoon," the thesis upon which this book is based.

Gabor Peterdi, printmaker and teacher, who guided the author in the development and simplification of some of the techniques presented in this book.

My wife, whose patience during the hundreds of hours of physical preparation of the original manuscript was of immeasurable importance.

And the children, without whose effort this book would have been impossible.

introduction

We are living in one of the most exciting and creative periods of graphic activity in Western culture. Thousands of artists all over the world are deeply involved in all phases of print making. Nowhere is this development more explosive than in the United States. Within the short period of a decade, the number of professional print makers has doubled, if not tripled. The number of major print shows and collections has increased at the same rate.

The development in print making unquestionably parallels the increased interest and activity in all phases of creative expression. Until now, however, the very useful discipline of print making was neglected on the elementary and high school levels of education. The same holds true in adult education. The primary reason behind this neglect is the still-existing confusion about prints in the mind of the general public. Both teachers and students are reluctant to get involved in something which they consider too complex, too technical, and too expensive.

Print making can be simple or complex. The degree of technical involvement should be directly related to the creative process. Complexity of technique is not synonymous with quality. Great prints can be created by the simplest of means. The Gothic woodcuts and some of the Matisse linocuts are ample proof of this.

Of all the graphic techniques, the surface printing methods are the most direct, and require the least amount of tools and special equipment. For this reason they are ideal to introduce children or nonprofessional adults to print making. There has been a need in the literature on print making for a book specifically written for this audience.

This book written by Norman Gorbaty fulfills that need. This treatise of surface printing methods is written with simplicity and clarity, and I am sure that it will help to introduce many children and adults to the exciting experience of creating a printed image.

GABOR PETERDI

general information

basic tools and materials

The tools and materials you will use most often are listed and described in this chapter. Additional materials for specific prints are described in the chapter covering the particular printmaking process. Check the list of materials given for the print you are planning to make. You will find that most of them are readily available in the home or in local stores.

THE WOODEN SPOON
An ordinary wooden mixing spoon is your printing press. Any store that sells kitchenware has them. Do not use a metal spoon. The rubbing necessary during printing generates so much heat that a metal spoon may get too hot to hold.

CARDBOARD FOR BACKING
Heavy cardboard is best for backing. Art stores usually carry a large selection in many colors.

CRAYONS
Heavy black crayons are best.

CUTTING TOOLS
Cutting tools should be kept clean and sharp. The sharper the tool, the slighter the chance of slipping. To prevent rusting, oil your tools before

you put them away. Most art and hobby shops carry the tools described in this chapter.

Never use a razor blade for cutting. A razor blade is awkward to handle, slips easily, and is dangerous even when used by a person experienced in handling it. A razor blade is recommended only for scraping the waxcut print block.

Woodcarving tools. A good set of woodcarving tools provides the best all-around cutting instruments for all relief blocks. These tools are comparatively inexpensive, considering the number of different graphic processes for which they can be used. They usually include a cutting knife, V-shaped gougers, U-shaped gougers, and flat chisels or gauges. The cutting knife is the most generally useful of all the tools. The V-shaped gougers are for fine detail work and the U-shaped gougers are useful for clearing away large areas and making broad lines. The flat chisel or gauge

A set of woodcarving tools.   _A set of linocut tools._

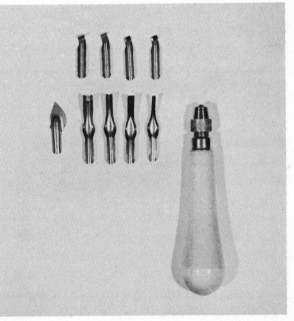

is used for smoothing surfaces. A standard set of woodcarving tools is illustrated in this chapter.

Linocut tools. A linocut set costs less than a woodcarving set but the tools cannot be used on hard materials such as wood. Some linocut sets come with interchangeable points in a variety of shapes and sizes. These points, which can usually be bought separately, eliminate the sharpening problem, for dull or broken blades can be replaced at small cost. Linocut tools come in "push" and "pull" types. The pull tools do not cut as fast as the push types; but since they are less apt to slip, they are more desirable when young children are working without supervision. A linocut set is illustrated in this chapter.

Knives. A good cutting knife comes with the set of woodcarving tools. However, other cutting knives can be used; art and hobby stores carry a wide selection. Ask for a Japanese cutting knife, probably the best knife for relief printmaking.

Scissors. Use a good pair of sharp desk scissors. Dull or small scissors are inefficient.

FOUNTAIN BRUSH
The fountain brush is now in common use for many purposes and can be bought in art and stationery stores under various trade names. It consists of a felt nib and a hollow holder filled with a special ink. The ink feeds down to the nib at just the right rate for easy use and dries almost instantly.

GLUE
White-resin glue and casein glue. **Either** one of these glues will do an equally good job. They can be bought ready to use, under various trade names, at hardware stores and lumber yards. Being creamy in consistency, they brush on easily. Since they are water-based, and oil and water do not mix, these glues make excellent sizing for printing blocks when oil-base inks are used. In addition to acting as sizing, they act as strengtheners because they dry to a clear, tough, plastic-like surface which forms a hard shell. Loose matter on the block, which might otherwise be picked up by the roller during inking, is secured by the glue shell. Be sure to get a wide glue brush.

INK

Oil-base inks are best for relief printing, with certain exceptions such as the potato print. Art stores carry small tubes, but larger tubes of superior quality can be bought from a printer or graphic supply house.

Water-base inks are harder to handle and more expensive, but they have the advantage of washing off readily with soap and water. However, they do tend to dry out rapidly. If ink dries on the block during printing, the print will tear as it is pulled from the block.

These inks come in black and in colors. Try printing with colored inks. Use the same block you used for the black ink. Wash the block, then over-print with color. Or use color alone. Try as many combinations as your imagination suggests. Rich effects can be achieved.

INKING SLAB

A good inking slab should be smooth and flat. Plate glass about $\frac{1}{4}''$ thick, with smooth edges, makes an excellent slab. Linoleum or formica glued to $\frac{7}{8}''$ plywood is often used. Lithostone works well, too. The slab should provide plenty of surface for rolling out a generous amount of ink. 14" x 14" is a good practical size. Always clean the inking slab after a series of printings, so the ink will not harden and collect dirt. Use turpentine to clean off oil-base inks. If you have used water-base ink, simply run water over the slab.

JIG

This is a device designed to prevent cutting tools from slipping during work on a cut-relief block. A jig is simple to construct and the cost of materials is trifling. See page 12 for directions and diagram.

NEWSPAPERS

Keep a stack of old newspapers handy. They are useful for protecting your working surface and for making cushioning pads, which are needed in some of the printing methods.

PRINTING SURFACES

Almost any kind of paper can be printed. Among the good easy-to-print papers that can be bought in any art store are newsprint paper (a wood-pulp paper), rice paper (mulberry paper) and finger-painting paper (a clay-coated paper). The finger-painting paper can be printed on either the shiny, coated side or on the dull side; each side will give a different quality to the print. Many other papers and surfaces can be printed, for example, paper toweling, shelving paper, and fabrics such as cotton, silk, or burlap. Each printing surface has something different to contribute to the print. You will find it challenging to explore the wide possibilities presented by different textured papers.

ROLLERS

Gelatine rollers. A good gelatine roller is the best roller for relief printing, unless you are using water-base ink. Because of its softness, this roller can get into crevices and low spots. However, it does require considerable care to keep it in good condition. It is very sensitive to temperature and to pressure. If left lying on a table for any length of time it will flatten; it should always be hung free, with no part of the gelatine rolling area touching anything. *Never use a gelatine roller when you are using water-base ink;* the water will undermine the gelatine surface of the roller and ruin it. Keep your roller clean so ink and dirt will not collect and create an uneven surface. Clean it with turpentine.

The fine prints that result from the use of the gelatine roller are well worth the extra care. This roller is the kind most used by professionals.

Rubber rollers. You will need a rubber roller if you use water-base inks. The rubber roller is tougher and easier to care for than the gelatine roller. And it costs less. Although it will not give the same fine quality prints possible with the gelatine roller, its sturdiness is an advantage in situations where special care is not practical, such as group work. However, if you want good prints, keep the roller clean. Water-base inks can be washed off under the faucet. Oil-base inks must be cleaned off with turpentine. If possible, hang your rubber roller free, too, when it is not in use. This will keep it in better condition, for a longer time.

TURPENTINE AND RAGS

A bottle or can of turpentine from the paint store and some soft rags are necessary for clean-up purposes. It is a good idea to throw away turpentine-soaked rags after they have been used to prevent any possibility of fire caused by spontaneous combustion.

how to make a jig

2"

7/8" 7/8"

Side view

2"

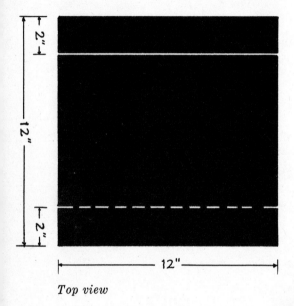

2"

12"

2"

12"

Top view

You can make a jig with three pieces of wood cut to size at a lumber yard. Get a piece of board 12"x12" and two strips 2"x⅞"x12". Nail one of the strips across one end of the board, placing the 2" dimension flat on the board. In the same way, nail the other strip to the underside of the opposite end of the board. That's all there is to making a jig.

The jig should be placed flat on the table so that the under strip catches on the edge of the table, holding the jig firmly in place. The raised strip at the upper end of the jig becomes a support to hold the block in place.

The use of a jig makes cutting easier and safer in all cut-relief methods. Always use a jig when cutting hard materials such as wood.

The jig in use

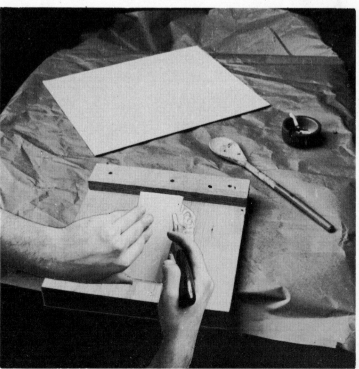

how to cut a block

The pictures below show the proper way to cut a block for relief printing. The basic principle illustrated is true for any of the relief processes.

How the cutting tool is held and how the block is fitted into the jig.

Cross section of a block after it has been correctly cut. Notice that the sides of the cuts are at an angle, similar to a pyramid. The corners of these areas will not break down during printing.

The proper way to hold the knife in relation to the area that is to print.

Cross section of a single cut, showing the correct angle.

The Wrong Way

Cross section of a badly cut block. The edges of these printing areas will break down in printing.

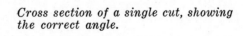

Cross section of a very badly cut block. These edges will break down even sooner.

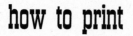

how to print

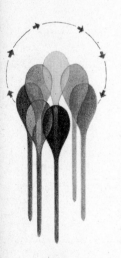

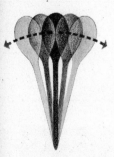

Before you start, protect your working table with layers of old newspapers. Arrange your printing materials conveniently. You will need your prepared block, printing paper, roller, ink, and inking slab. Squeeze a small quantity of ink on the inking slab. The ink must be "worked out" by rolling the roller back and forth over the ink; add more ink from time to time. Raise the roller from the ink after each stroke, spinning the roller so that every part of it will be evenly inked (Illustration 1). When the roller is well inked you are ready to ink your block. The block is inked by running the roller back and forth over the surface (Illustration 2). When you are satisfied that every part of the block is properly inked, move the block, inked side up, to a spot safely away from the ink and inking slab. Put a piece of printing paper over the block. Smooth out the paper gently with the side of your hand, rubbing very lightly. This is important because the ink will then act as an adhesive between the paper and the block, thereby holding the paper in place during printing.

Now you are ready to use the wooden spoon as a printing press. As a further precaution against slipping, hold the printing paper down with one hand. Hold the wooden spoon in the other (Illustration 3). Place your forefinger in the bowl of the spoon. Rub the paper with the spoon, using a circular back-and-forth movement while applying pressure with the forefinger. Move over the entire surface of the block in this way. Be sure you have rubbed over every part of the paper that touches the block. When the entire area has been rubbed the print will be ready to "pull." Pulling a print simply means taking it off the printing block. Do this very carefully. But first check to see if the print is ready to be "pulled." Slowly lift one corner of the paper (Illustration 4). If this corner does not look properly printed, lift the entire side, about one-half of the paper, and roll more ink on the exposed part of the block. Replace the paper carefully and repeat the same procedure on the other side. Rub with the wooden spoon again, very gently. Then "pull" your print and there is your picture. If the first inspection of the corner of the print shows that the inking and printing is satisfactory, the print can be taken off the block, or "pulled," immediately.

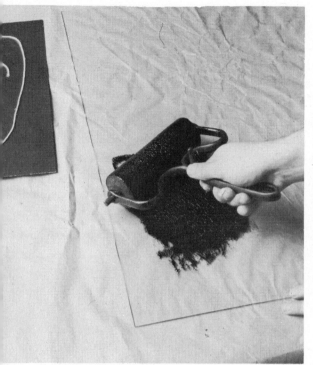

1 *Inking the roller.*

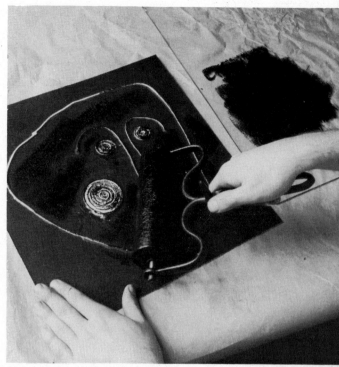

2 *Inking the block.*

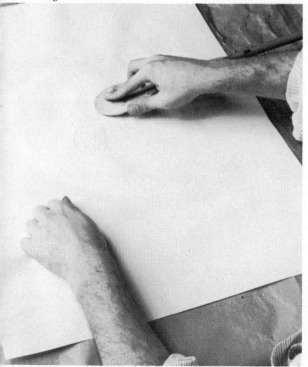

3 *Printing with a spoon.*

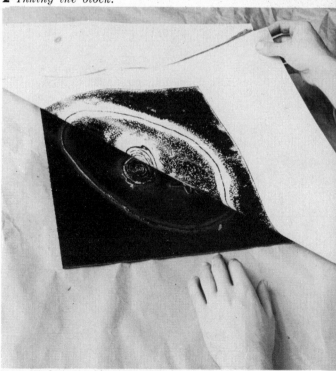

4 *Checking a corner of the print for inking quality.*

2

bean print

If you can glue you can make a bean print. It is probably the simplest of all the relief processes. Beans and grains are glued on a piece of cardboard to form a design. When the gluing procedure is finished the design will be firmly cemented to the cardboard and you will have a block ready for printing.

The design is not sketched on the block. It is constructed directly with beans, one bean at a time. The beans are arranged and organized to build a picture. Proper placement of every bean must be given consideration, for each bean is as important to the picture as a whole as each brick is to a house. The beans make the lines and areas formed by this method look dotted, and the finished print will have a distinctive dot appearance unlike any other relief print.

Making a bean block is a leisurely occupation, relaxing for adults and absorbing for children; I have seen children as young as four years engrossed by work on bean prints for unbelievably long stretches, sometimes two and three hours at a time.

basic tools and materials

Wooden spoon

Cardboard for backing,
  preferably a dark color or black

White resin glue or casein glue

Glue brush—wide (about ½")

Ink

Inking slab

Roller

Printing paper

Turpentine and rags

additional materials

Beans and grains
  Lima beans, lentils, split peas, rice, barley, chick peas, black-eyed beans, and so forth. Get a variety. They cost very little at any grocery store. Large units, such as the flat-sided lima beans, are the easiest to handle and the most satisfactory for the main elements of the design. The small grains are hard to handle as units, but you will need them for backgrounds and textural effects.

Bowls
  A separate deep bowl to hold each kind of bean and grain is a great convenience. A shallower bowl that won't tip over easily will be useful for the glue.

Medium sandpaper
  Paint and art stores carry this.

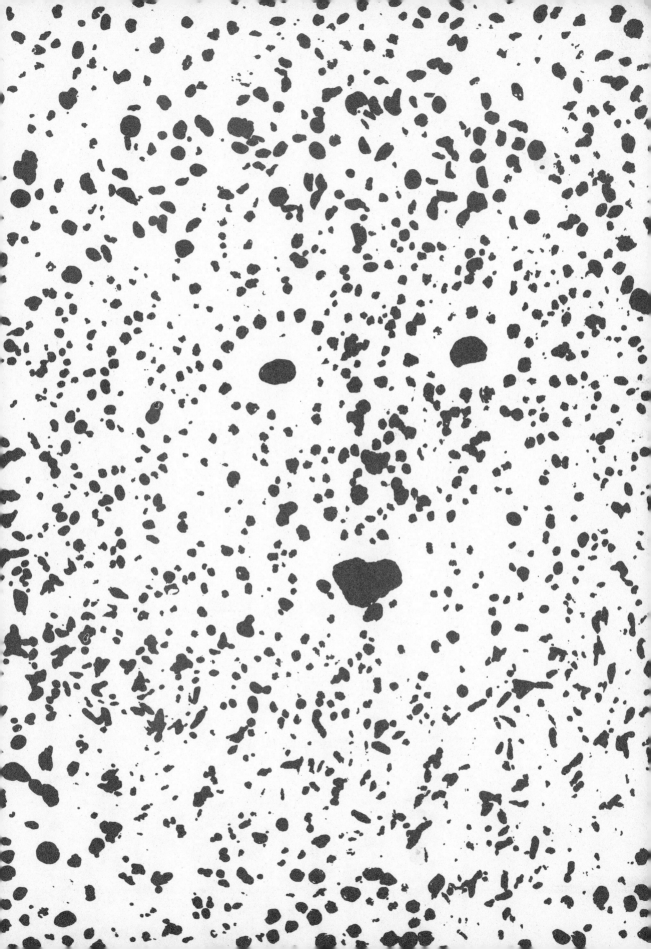

how to make the block

Cut the cardboard to the size you want the finished print to be. Place the beans and grains you plan to use in individual bowls. Pour glue into the shallow bowl.

Begin by deciding where the first bean is to go. You will find that lima beans are the easiest to handle. With the glue brush, put a thick puddle of glue on the cardboard. The thicker the puddle, the better the final bonding action. Place a lima bean flat side down in the glue puddle. Place the next lima bean in another glue puddle. Continue in this way, planning your design step-by-step as you go. When the basic design is completed you will be ready to put in backgrounds, if desired, and textural effects with the small grains. To do this, cover the area with a thick coat of glue and sprinkle grains on the glue. Tip the cardboard so that any loose grains will fall off. If more grains are needed to get the effect you have in mind, resprinkle and tip the block again.

When the design is finished, set it aside to dry for at least five hours. When it is dry, apply a coat of glue over the entire block, right on top of

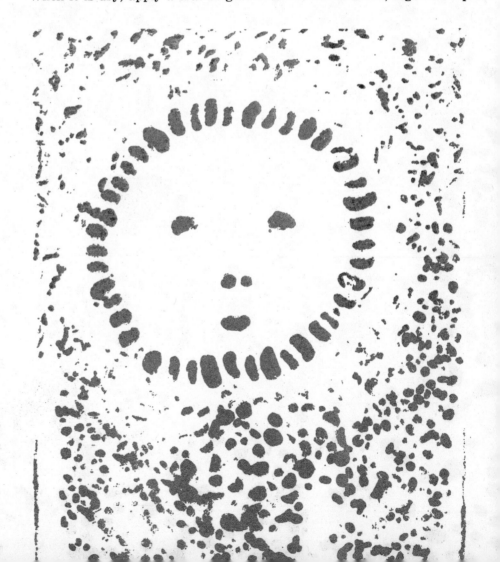

the beans. After this coat of glue has dried the block must be sandpapered. Sanding is of prime importance in the making of a successful bean print. It will remove any loose matter which might otherwise come off during printing and spoil the print. It will produce a flatter printing surface and improve the adhesive action of the ink during printing. This adhesive action holds the paper in position. Because the bean print has only a small area to take up ink, the adhesive or holding action of the ink is reduced. Careful sanding and heavy inking are necessary to strengthen this action in order to keep the paper from slipping while it is being printed.

After sandpapering, wipe off the block with a clean cloth to remove any dust. The bean block is now ready for printing.

Applying a puddle of glue to the spot on which the bean will be placed.

how to print

Proceed according to the general printing instructions in Chapter 1. Be sure to remember that the bean print requires heavy inking. The more ink you roll on the block, the easier it will be to print the picture and the better the print will be.

Sandpapering the block.

Pulling the print.

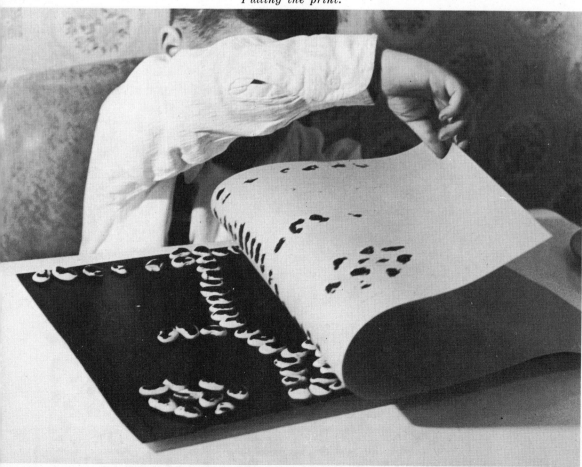

3

string print

The string print method is a simple one. Pieces of string are glued to a piece of cardboard. This piece of cardboard becomes the block from which you print pictures.

Direct and elementary as it is, the string print has, however, an unusual value. It exposes the mind to an entirely new concept in which string is used as a drawing medium, instead of pen or pencil. You draw pictures directly with string, without any previously drawn guide, gluing the string to the cardboard as you "draw." Instead of a pencil line you have a string line. This is a new idea and a challenge. You'll find it's fun, too. With a handful of string and a piece of cardboard you can enjoy a new means of creative expression.

Notice that the string print reproduced opposite shows a "glow" or halo around the line. This halo is characteristic of most shallow prints because their relief surface is low and therefore, during the inking process, the roller inks most of the background as well as the design. As a rule, only a narrow area between the raised relief surface and the block will be left free of ink. This, then, is the only part of the block that will not print. The result is the narrow white line or halo surrounding the design.

basic tools and materials

Wooden spoon	Inking slab
Cardboard for backing, *black or a dark color*	Printing paper
Glue: white resin or casein glue	Roller
Glue brush: wide (about ½″)	Scissors
Ink	Turpentine and rags

additional materials

String
> *Almost any kind of string can be used, but lintless string is probably the best. It is usually stronger and has a certain stiffness which makes it easier to handle than other types of string.*

Airplane cement or model-builders' cement
> *These are the best glues for cementing the string to the block. They come in tubes, ready to use, and can be bought in hardware stores, ten-cent stores, and hobby shops.*

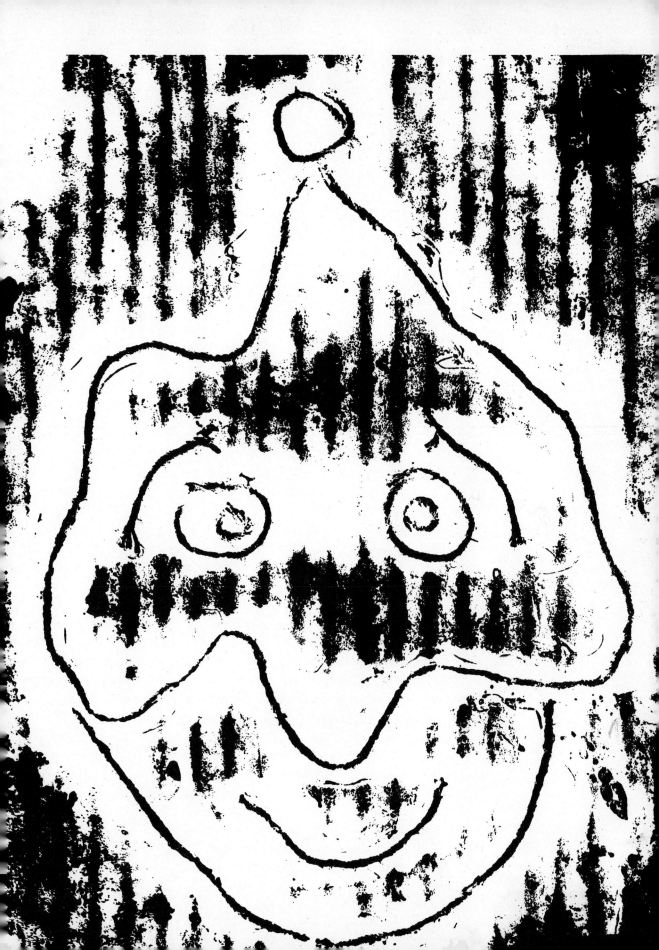

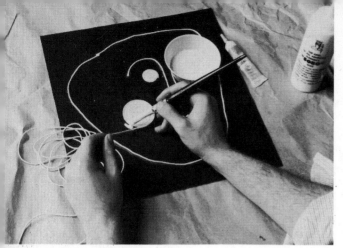

Applying glue to the area on which the string will be placed.

Cutting the string.

how to make the block

Keep in mind the idea of "drawing with string" and begin your block. First cut the cardboard backing the size of the print you want. Then place varying lengths of string on it. Move and twist these pieces of string around until an idea for a design takes form. This handling of the string will give you a familiarity with its qualities. You will soon discover that the string line cannot be controlled as completely as a pencil line. However, it can be handled, cut, moved from place to place, felt, glued. It has an integrity of its own, for string will only let itself be bent in certain ways. Forcing it will result in a poor print. Observe the natural direction the string likes to take and avoid unlikely positions.

As a specific line is decided on, cut the string to the proper length. Differing widths of string can be used to make lines of different widths. Place the string in position on the cardboard and squeeze a drop of airplane or model builders cement on the string. Be sure that the cement covers the string from one side of its width to the other. Repeat this cementing along the entire length of the string in as many places as possible, to insure a strong bond. Try to keep the string as flat as possible. Continue this procedure throughout the development of your string picture. When all the string lines in your design have been cemented into position, set the block aside to let the cement harden. When the cement is dry and hard, give the entire block a coat of white resin or casein glue, over the string. This coating of glue will prevent lint from coming off during inking and printing and will also give greater strength to the cement bond between the string and the block. Allow the coat of glue to dry until it is hard to the touch. Then apply another coat over the entire block. Put the block aside for at least three hours. By that time the glue coating will be thoroughly dry and set, and the block will be ready for printing.

how to print

The string print is printed in the same manner as most relief prints. Follow the general printing instructions in Chapter 1. Be sure to ink the block heavily. The string print has less relief surface than most relief prints, so it requires more ink to keep the paper from slipping during printing.

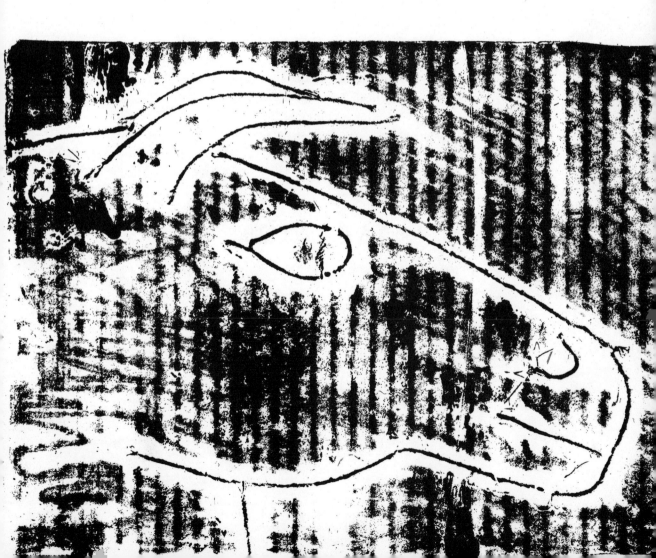

4

cardboard print

Almost everyone likes to cut and paste; and this easy print block can be made by simply cutting shapes out of thin cardboard and pasting them on heavy cardboard. Pictures and designs are composed by arrangements of these shapes. The resulting prints have a very attractive look—a white halo silhouettes black shapes against a black background.

The cardboard print is a shallow print, like the string print, and therefore most of the background, as well as the design, will take up ink and print. Usually only a narrow area around the pasted-down shapes will remain entirely uninked. This area will not print and so forms the interesting halo.

In this method you draw with scissors. Shapes for your design are cut directly out of cardboard, without a previously drawn guide. And since cardboard is not suitable for intricate cutting with scissors, you learn to express your ideas in uncomplicated forms. For variety and special effects, use textured cardboard. Different textures will produce different qualities of black when printed.

The cardboard print is another new language for self expression, another different technique that develops originality. The materials are inexpensive and easy to handle. It takes very little time and skill to make pleasing prints by this method.

basic tools and materials

Wooden spoon

Cardboard backing:
white or a light color

Scissors

Glue: white resin or casein

Ink

Inking slab

Roller

Printing paper

Turpentine, newspapers and rags

additional materials

Thin cardboard
This should be thin enough to be readily cut into simple outline shapes with scissors. Poster board or "railroad board," available at any art store, are both fine for the purpose. Black or a dark color will show up best on a light background. Textured cardboard can be used to give varying qualities of black to the finished print.

Rubber cement, instead of glue, if you prefer
If you decide to make your block with rubber cement, you will not need the glue listed above. Glue should never be used with rubber cement.

how to make the block

Cutting the cardboard to the desired shapes.

First cut the heavy cardboard backing to the size of the print you want. This is the background on which you will paste cut-out shapes. Have your total picture in mind before you start to cut the individual shapes. Decide on the shape of the first piece you plan to paste down. Using the thin cardboard, cut out this shape directly with scissors; do not draw it. Do not plan to use too many small shapes; they are apt to fall off the block. The larger the shape, the better it will stick.

After you have cut a few shapes, start pasting. The shapes should be pasted down one at a time. Select the proper spot for the first one. Cover the spot with a thick coat of glue. Gently press the cut-out piece on the glue and hold it down firmly for a few seconds, to make sure it sticks. Continue cutting and pasting in this way until your design is complete.

When every cut-out shape is in place, cover the entire block with a coat of glue. Let it dry. When the first coat of glue is dry, apply a second coat. These glue coats protect the pasted-down shapes so that they will stay flat during the printing process. Let the block stand for at least a day. When it is thoroughly dry and set, it is ready for printing.

If you use rubber cement instead of glue, the pasting procedure is different. You must put a coat of rubber cement on both the cut-out piece and the section of the backing where it will be placed. Allow both to dry for a full minute before putting them together. Then place the coated side of the cut-out piece on the coated section of the backing. Cover with newspaper and apply pressure by a slow rubbing motion with the side of your hand. Remove the newspaper. If there is any excess rubber cement left on the block, rub it vigorously with your fingers; it will roll off neatly. This method of cementing usually creates a strong bond. However, if a piece loosens, simply re-cement it. *Do not cover the block with glue.* Never use glue with rubber cement. A block prepared with rubber cement dries quickly. After an hour or so your block will be ready for printing.

Gluing the cut cardboard shapes to the heavy cardboard block.

how to print

The cardboard print block is inked and printed in the same manner as most relief prints. Follow the general printing instructions in Chapter 1.

5

drip print

Here is a print block you can make without cutting or gluing. Thick lacquer is dripped on cardboard, Masonite, or wood. When the lacquer hardens, your print is finished.

Prints from these blocks have a striking individuality all their own. The tonal quality is grayish. Sprawling, uneven lines are formed by the dripping lacquer. There are almost no large areas of solid black because there are almost no areas that will take up ink evenly. Since the drip block is shallow like the string and cardboard block, white halos appear here and there.

Boldness of design is almost a necessity when making a drip print block. Complicated patterns cannot be achieved with dripping lacquer, so details must be eliminated and significant ideas broadly expressed in large shapes and wide lines. You will be surprised and pleased at how easily you can get arresting effects.

The drip print method is particularly suitable for large groups working on the same project at the same time because the procedure is simple and only a few inexpensive materials are needed.

basic tools and materials

Wooden spoon

Backing: cardboard, Masonite, or wood;
 white or a very light tone

Ink

Inking slab

Roller

Printing paper

Turpentine, newspapers and rags

additional materials

Lacquer
 The lacquer used for drip prints must be thick. Get the thickest grade your paint store carries. Lacquer can be thickened, if necessary, by letting the can stand open for a few hours. Exposure to air will evaporate some of the thinner.

Wooden sticks
 Flat popsicle sticks or medical tongue depressors, which can be bought in drugstores are the most satisfactory for dripping lacquer. But any short, flat stick will do.

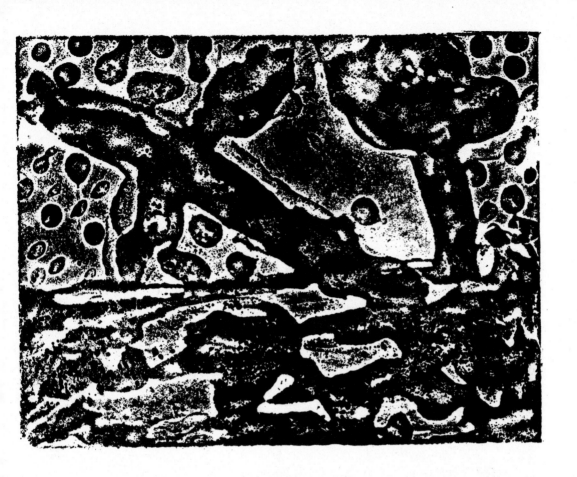

29

how to make the block

First experiment a little with the lacquer, to become accustomed to its behavior. When you are ready to make the actual block, cut the backing (cardboard, Masonite, or wood) to the desired shape and size. Do not draw a preliminary design on the backing—part of the fun is in drawing with the dripping lacquer.

Dip your flat stick about one-third of the way down into the can of lacquer and, while the stick is still dripping, begin your design. The stick can be held above the backing so that lacquer drips down, or the stick can touch the backing and be used as a drawing instrument. Unless the lacquer is very thick it will be necessary to repeat dripping on top of the lines already formed, in order to build up the level of the lacquer. If the level is not high enough the entire block will print black. The lacquer should be about the thickness of thin cardboard, such as matchbook cardboard.

After the lacquer design is completed, the block is finished. Set it aside to dry overnight. When the lacquer is thoroughly hard, the block is ready for printing.

how to print

The drip print is printed in the same manner as most relief prints. Follow the printing instructions in Chapter 1.

Applying the lacquer with a flat stick.   *Inking the block.*

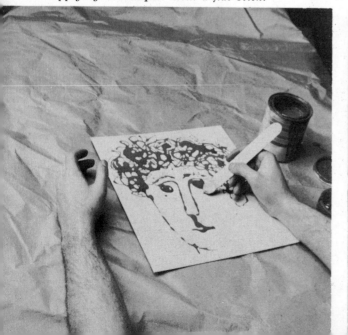

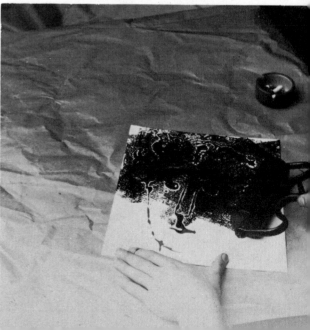

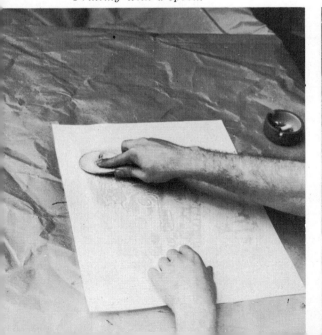

Printing with a spoon.

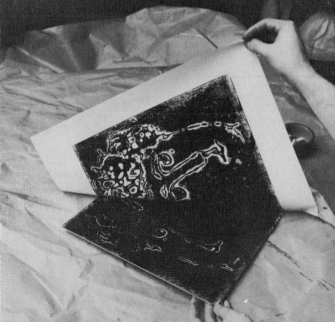

Pulling the print.

6

paper print

If you draw a design on heavy paper and cut away all the background, you will have a paper surface ready to print with. The cut-out design is not attached to a backing, as in most relief processes; it is used for printing just as it is. Actually the paper surface is a kind of stencil-in-reverse: areas that are to be printed are left intact while areas that are not to print are cut away. The intact area becomes the relief surface that will be inked and used for printing pictures. In other words, it is very much like cutting out paper dolls and using them to print pictures of paper dolls.

Paper prints have a bold silhouette look, much like linoleum prints. There is very little texture in the prints, unless textured paper is used, and very little detail, for it is hard to cut detailed designs and they do not stand up well in printing.

Although basically the paper print is one of the simplest of all the relief processes and uses only the simplest materials, this print presents a series of interesting problems in design, cutting, and printing. Developing ingenuity in solving such problems, how to attach borders, for example, or how to devise patterns that will not be torn by the roller, is part of learning how to create within the limitations of the medium.

The paper print is an excellent process for group work.

basic tools and materials

Wooden spoon	Inking slab
Crayon	Roller
Cutting knife or scissors	Printing paper
Ink	Turpentine, newspapers and rags

additional materials

Stencil paper
Brown stencil paper or heavy frisket paper (which is an oiled stencil paper), are thoroughly dependable materials for making paper prints. They cut easily, yet are strong enough to stand up under the strain of printing. Other papers can be used, two-ply bristol board, for instance, which is thin enough to cut and strong enough to be used for printing. These papers can be bought in art stores. Experiment with other papers; you may make some interesting discoveries. Textured papers will give variation to the quality of the blacks in the print.

how to make the block

Before making the print block, practice with the kind of paper you are going to use. Draw pictures and cut them out to see just what kind of shapes are practical. Draw with a heavy crayon so the lines will be easy to follow with a cutting knife or scissors. Scissors are suitable only if the design is very simple. If you plan to have a border around your picture you must be careful to see that the design and the border are attached. If this is not done, the picture will fall out of the border.

Once the drawing is finished you are ready to cut. But first cover your work table with layers of newspaper or a sheet of Masonite, to protect the surface. If you use a cutting knife be sure to hold it according to the instructions in Chapter 1, on how to cut a block. All cutting should be done slowly and carefully. If a knife is being used, cut just deep enough to break the surface of the paper. Then you can pull away the background, leaving only the piece of paper that is your design. Be sure to trim edges clean. When your design is completely cut out and all the background neatly trimmed away, it is a relief block ready for printing.

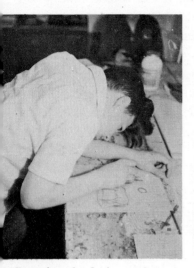

Drawing the design on heavy paper.

Cutting out the design with a sharp cutting knife.

Inking the block. Be sure to roll from the center out so that the paper will not tear.

how to print

The procedure for inking and printing a paper print is somewhat different from the usual relief printing method. First prepare your inking slab and roller according to the instructions in Chapter 1; use a great deal of ink.

Then lay the cut-out design on the inked slab. The cut-out must be inked with the roller while it is on the slab, because the ink, being sticky, will act as an adhesive agent and hold the cut-out in place. Because of its shape and nature, there is no other way to keep it flat and firm. In addition, a certain amount of ink will attach to the underside; this is important later in the printing process.

Carefully roll the inked roller over the paper cut-out, rolling from the center out toward the edges. Rolling in this way will reduce the risk of tearing the cut-out or having it stick to the roller.

When the cut-out is well inked, it is ready to be taken off the inking slab. To do this, use the edge of a knife to lift one corner. Then you can catch the corner with your fingers and lift the entire piece, slowly and carefully. This way it won't tear.

Place the cut-out on a clean sheet of paper. The side that was inked with the roller should be up. The ink on the underside, picked up from the slab, will help to make it stick flat to the clean sheet of paper and prevent slipping during the printing.

Now you are ready to print. Put a piece of printing paper over the inked cut-out design. Smooth out the printing paper gently with the side of your hand, pressing lightly to make it stick. Next, while holding the printing paper down with one hand, rub the surface with the wooden spoon according to the instructions in Chapter 1.

When the rubbing is completed, the print is ready to be "pulled." Only, in this case, when you "pull" your print, instead of taking your print off the block, you must take your block off the print. Starting with one corner, slowly lift the printing paper. You will find the cut-out design stuck to it. Again, using the edge of a knife to raise a corner, carefully pull the cut-out design off the printing paper. Put it to one side. It can be used again to make more prints. You will find your design printed on the printing paper. This is your finished print.

7
potato print

Most of us remember the excitement, when we were children, of cutting initials into a potato and using it as a stamp to "print." Primitive as those prints were, the principle was sound. The final image on paper was printed from a raised surface created by cutting away areas that were not supposed to print. This is the basic principle of all cut-relief prints. The design can be cut out of the block, leaving the background as the raised printing surface. This results in a white design on a black background. Or the background can be cut away from the design, resulting in a black design on a white background. In either case the design is created by printing on a raised, or relief, surface.

Potato prints are probably the simplest and best introduction to cut relief printmaking. It is easy to carve the soft surface of a freshly cut potato. Results can be seen almost immediately after cutting, for the prints are made by stamping, and stamping is the least complicated of all printing methods. The potato is handled the same way as a rubber stamp. Just slide the potato block over ink and start stamping out your pictures.

There are a number of ways of picture-making with a potato. The easiest way of all is to simply alter the outside shape of the potato-half. Another way is to carve a design out of the surface; the background will be the shape of a potato. Or cut away the background and leave the design to print. These methods can be used singly or in various combinations. All-over patterns can be made by repeatedly stamping the same block. A series of blocks can be organized to make one picture.

The potato, being vegetable matter, will disintegrate in a comparatively short time. But potatoes are inexpensive, and the process is easy; so just carve another block if your potato breaks down.

basic tools and materials

Cutting tools	Rubber roller
Water-base ink	Printing paper
Inking slab	Newspapers and rags

additional materials

Potatoes
The larger the potato the easier it will be to handle and work with. Idaho pota-toes are ideal because of their shape and size.

how to make the block

Wash the potatoes and cut them in half. Try to make the cut as smooth as possible because this will end up as the printing surface. Each potato-half will make one block. You can experiment with inking and printing a half potato before cutting a design, if you wish. Or cut along the outside edge, for cutting practice. To do this, lay the potato-half, cut side down, on a piece of paper and cut into the sides with vertical strokes of the cutting knife. Make border patterns, or a simple large shape, such as a heart or half-moon. These shapes will print solid black.

After a little initial practice you will be ready to cut into the surface of the potato. If you cut the design out of the potato, use the scoopers and gougers. If you cut away the background and leave the design intact, use the cutting knife and follow the general instructions, Chapter 1, on how to cut a block.

how to print

The procedure is different from the inking and printing of most relief blocks. Potato blocks are the only relief blocks printed by stamping. Water-base inks must be used. Although oil-base inks are generally recommended

Cutting the design into the surface of the potato block.

Inking the block.

Making the print.

for relief printing, they cannot be used for printing potato blocks, since potatoes contain water, and oil and water do not mix. Water-base inks, usually rather hard to handle because they tend to dry out on the block, are easy to use with the potato block, for the water in the potato will thin out the ink during the printing. They also have the advantage of washing off readily with water and soap.

Before you start, spread your printing paper over a thick pad of old newspapers. This pad forms a cushion that makes it easier to get good impressions when you stamp. Now put plenty of the ink on your inking slab and even it out. You can do this with a rubber roller, but never use a gelatine roller with water-base ink. Do not use a roller to ink the potato block. The potato is too small to be satisfactorily inked in this way. Instead, put the potato, cut side down, on the inking slab and slide it around until it picks up enough ink to make a print. Now pick up the potato and place it inked side down on the printing paper. Press down firmly. Lift the block and see if you have a good impression. Re-ink the block after making each impression before stamping again.

8

waxcut print

A block of ordinary paraffin wax is the base for this print. It is an excellent follow-up for the potato print. If you have made a potato print, you are now familiar with many of the principles of cut relief printmaking even though the potato print is unusual in some respects. The waxcut print employs all the standard procedures used in most cut relief prints, yet the wax is so easy to cut into that the cutting itself presents no problem.

It is best to cut the design directly into the block. Preliminary drawing is not practical. Ink or crayon will not take on the wax, and a pencil, when used as a guide, will make impressions that show on the final print. However, the wax being soft, it is possible to make good simple waxcut prints by using a hard pencil as a cutting tool instead of as a drawing tool.

Broad angular patterns are typical of the finished print. The black areas have a characteristic texture produced by razor blade or knife marks made while leveling the block, and by air bubbles in the wax itself which show up as white dots.

The waxcut is a new medium, and it offers an easy new way to learn how to cut a relief block properly.

basic tools and materials

Wooden spoon

Cutting tools:
  gougers and scoopers are the most useful

Jig

Ink

Inking slab

Roller

Printing paper

Turpentine, newspapers, and rags

additional materials

Household wax
  Household wax, or paraffin, usually comes in a package containing four blocks, each 5" x 2½". Buy it in any grocery or hardware store. It costs very little.

Single-edge razor blade
  This is to be used for scraping, only. It is not recommended for cutting the block.

how to make the block

The block needs to be prepared a day in advance because it must be inked and dry before you can start work on it. The first step in the preparation is to smooth the wax by scraping the surface with a single-edge razor blade or a knife. Next, roll a heavy coat of ink on the smoothed surface. This black ink coating will make it easy to see what you are doing when you start to cut your design. Let the block stand overnight so the ink will dry hard.

The next day, when the ink is thoroughly dry, the block can be cut. Cutting will be easier if you use a jig (page 12). Fit the block into the jig, with the inked side up. Have your picture in mind and start cutting. The cutting knife will not be very useful for the waxcut block; the V-shaped gouger can be used for making fine lines and the U-shaped scooper or

Inking the block for printing.

The finished block, ready to print.

Pulling the print.

gouger for clearing away large areas and for making wide lines. The cuts need not be very deep, but make them carefully so the sides will not break down in printing. You will appreciate the black coating on the block now. Every cut you make into the block will reveal the white wax. The white part will not print; the parts left black, will. When you have finished cutting you will be able to see your design clearly in black-and-white right on the block, before printing.

how to print

The waxcut print is inked and printed in the same manner as most relief prints. Follow the printing instructions in Chapter 1.

mo-glu print

This is a fascinating new process and it is lots of fun. Its name comes from the two chief ingredients used in preparing the block—molasses and rabbit-skin glue. These two ingredients are combined to make a gelatine-like substance called mo-glu. The process, developed elsewhere, was successfully introduced at the Smith Day School in Northampton, Massachusetts, by Prof. George Swinton.

The block consists of a piece of glass coated with the mo-glu. Designs are cut into the coating and those areas not to be printed are stripped off. This results in a block with a raised design. The design can be cut directly into the mo-glu without using a cutting guide or the design can first be drawn lightly on the surface of the coating. Another way is to place a crayon drawing under the block. The block is semi-transparent, so the drawing will be seen clearly enough to serve as a cutting guide.

The most successful mo-glu print designs use large, simple areas with a minimum of detail. Since the surface of the block is smooth, there is very little texture in the finished prints. If you want texture in any part of the print, you can drip extra mo-glu mixture on the surface after the original coat has hardened.

Stripping off areas not to be printed, instead of cutting or gouging them away, is an entirely new way of producing a relief surface for printing. And, like the other new methods in this book, it has its own interesting new problems to solve.

basic tools and materials

Wooden spoon

Cutting knife

Oil-base ink
Never use water-base inks with mo-glu blocks, because they will destroy the water-soluble coating.

Inking slab

Rubber roller
Do not use a gelatine roller for this process.

Printing paper

Turpentine, newspapers, and rags

additional materials

Rabbit-skin glue
This glue comes in cans or cardboard containers in dried granular form, and can be bought in most art stores. Be sure directions for use are on the container.

Molasses
Get the smallest bottle your grocery carries. That will be plenty.

Concentrated fruit pectin
Most grocery stores carry 8-ounce bottles of this under several different brand names.

Double boiler

Plate glass for the background
You will need a piece of plate glass about the size of the print you plan to make. It should be ¼" thick, with polished edges. Your local glass store will cut this for you.

how to make the block

Before starting the block, the gelatine-like mo-glu must be prepared; it is an overnight process. Pour a pound of the dried glue into the top of a double boiler and add water according to the directions on the glue container. This mixture must stand overnight. The next morning, stir to make sure the glue is completely dissolved, then heat it in the double boiler to just below the boiling point, but do not let it boil. Remove from the heat and add three or four tablespoonfuls of molasses, according to the thickness of the molasses, which varies. Stir thoroughly. The mixture should be "molassesy" in consistency. If the consistency seems right, it is ready to pour on the glass background.

If possible, place your glass background near an open window. The air

will speed the jelling when you pour the mo-glu. Have plenty of newspapers under the glass, for the warm mo-glu usually overflows.

When everything is ready, pour mo-glu on the glass. It should jell within 30 seconds. Use your best judgment in deciding how much mo-glu to pour. More accuracy will come with experience. Don't worry about using too much because the mo-glu immediately touching the glass will jell rapidly and the excess mo-glu will run off. A jellied coating will be left on the block.

If the mo-glu does not jell in 30 seconds, wash it all off the block. Add a little fruit pectin to the batch of mo-glu still left in the double boiler. Stir. Now pour some of this on the block. As before, the excess will run off. If a coating of mo-glu jells firmly and clings to the block within 30 seconds, all is well.

When the mo-glu coating is properly jelled and set, the block is ready to cut. It should be dry and firm to the touch.

Cut the block by any of the three methods mentioned before; that is, draw lightly on the mo-glu and use the drawing as a guide for cutting, or cut a design directly into the mo-glu without a guide, or place a heavy-crayon drawing under the block to serve as a cutting guide. All the areas that are not to print must be stripped off. Do this by inserting the knife point under one corner of the mo-glu and lifting that corner so you can catch it with your fingers. Then peel away the unwanted mo-glu.

When the only mo-glu left on the block is the design, the block is ready for printing.

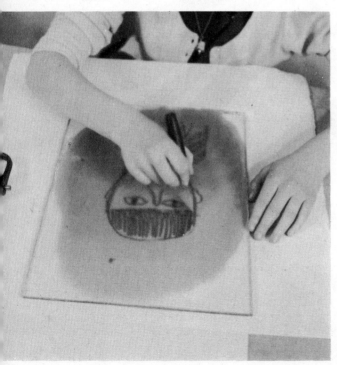

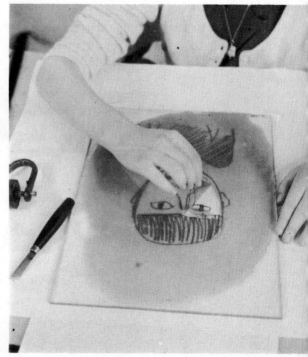

Cutting the design into the mo-glu surface with a cutting knife. Notice how clearly the crayon drawing under the block can be seen.

Peeling off the mo-glu after the design has been cut.

how to print

The mo-glu block is inked and printed in the same manner as most cut relief prints. Follow the printing instructions in Chapter 1.

corrugated cardboard print

Here is a good example of how to make a print block out of material found in almost every household.

With a piece of corrugated cardboard from a grocery box, you can make a print block that has tremendous flexibility for so simple a material. Corrugated cardboard usually consists of three layers of paper—two smooth sheets enclosing a corrugated sheet. With these three layers a whole series of different textures can be worked out. Where the top surface is left intact, it will print black. Where the second layer, the corrugated one, is exposed, a series of strong parallel lines will print. When you cut down to the last layer, removing the first and the second, this area won't print at all and will show as white on the print. By these means, you can design a print with black against black parallel lines, solid black on white, white on black, white against black parallel lines, or variations of these combinations.

With material as unassuming as corrugated cardboard, you can make prints that are striking in appearance and very impressive. They have power, and a bold, modernistic look.

Do not confuse this method with the cardboard print in an earlier chapter. The cardboard print is a cemented relief process, whereas the corrugated cardboard print is a true cut relief method.

basic tools and materials

Wooden spoon

Cutting knife

Glue:
  white resin or casein

Ink

Inking slab

Roller

Printing paper

Turpentine, newspapers, and rags

additional materials

Corrugated cardboard
  Any corrugated cardboard box can be used. Corrugated board can also be bought in art or stationery stores.

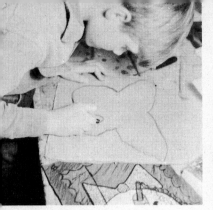
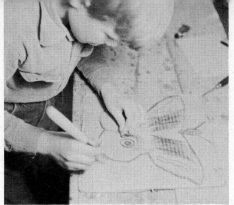

Drawing the design on the corrugated cardboard with a crayon.

Peeling off the top layer of cardboard after cutting.

Inking the block.

how to make the block

Cut the corrugated cardboard to the size and shape you want. This is your block, ready for the design. It needs no further preparation.

It is best to use the cutting knife as a drawing instrument. Drawing on corrugated board with a pencil or crayon and then trying to follow the lines with a knife is both difficult and unsatisfactory. You can trace your picture lightly with the knife point before cutting into the layers, if you wish. Keep the areas large and the lines wide.

Use a jig (page 12) and follow the cutting instructions in Chapter 1. Fit the block into the jig and then start your design. Cut slowly, keeping in mind that guiding a knife through corrugated cardboard takes as much care as cutting into harder material, such as linoleum.

If you want to make an area of parallel lines, cut the outline of the area just deep enough to pierce the top layer of the cardboard. Peel off this top layer by inserting the knife blade into a corner along the cut line and then lifting this corner so you can catch the paper with your fingers and strip it away. Sometimes the surface layer of paper will not peel off entirely. In this case, run a pencil along the furrows of the corrugation in order to break the thin paper that may be left. You can pull these small bits off with your fingers.

For any area that you want to be white on the print, cut the desired shape deep into the corrugated layer. If you cut deeply enough, both the cover-paper and the corrugated layer can be peeled off in one operation. Be sure no loose paper clings to the block.

All areas left intact will print black. Therefore, the two cutting-steps described above will give you three values on your finished print—white, solid black, and black parallel lines.

When all the cutting is finished, give the entire block a thin coat of glue. The glue will seal rough edges and act as a sizing agent to improve the printing surface. It will dry in about an hour. After the glue is dry, your block is ready for printing.

Checking a corner of the print.

how to print

The corrugated cardboard block is printed in the same manner as most relief prints. Follow the printing instructions in Chapter 1.

11

casein cut print

The casein cut print is a new process that employs all the techniques for true cut relief prints, yet offers the advantage of a surface that is particularly easy to cut into. It was developed by the author while working at the School of Art and Architecture at Yale University.

Preparing the block is an interesting procedure. A cutting surface is built up by painting layers of casein paint on a piece of Masonite. After the paint dries, it is dabbed with water which gives it the consistency of semi-hardened clay. You will find it wonderfully easy to cut a design into this. Then, too, it will dry to a hard firm surface that makes good prints.

While the surface is soft, you can press texture effects into it, if you wish. After it hardens you can sandpaper some parts for textural effect, leaving the parts you want solid-black unsandpapered. Often, the ridges in the background, created during scooping, will print, adding interest and character.

The casein cut is a simple cut-relief print process that requires a minimum of cutting skill, but can produce a variety of attractive prints, many of them resembling linocuts or woodcuts. You can prepare blocks in advance and store them until you are ready to cut and print. This is an added advantage if you are planning a group project.

basic tools and materials

Wooden spoon

Heavy crayon or a fountain brush

Cutting tools:
  gougers or scoopers will be especially useful

Jig

Ink

Inking slab

Roller

Printing paper

Turpentine, newspapers, and rags

additional materials

Water-base casein paint and a wide, paint brush
Buy the paint in a paint store. It is very economical compared to other kinds of paint. Be sure to specify water-base. This is important, for casein paint also comes rubber-based, and rubber-base types cannot be used for the casein block. The water-base casein paint will be pasty in the can. Thin it out with water to a creamy consistency before using.

Masonite
A large sheet of untempered Masonite can be bought and cut to the desired size at a lumber yard. It is important to get untempered Masonite because it has a high degree of absorbency which is necessary to create a bond between the casein paint and the block.

Deep bowls and water

Cloth
Pieces of cloth, about the size of small wash cloths, for dampening the casein block.

Sandpaper
You will need both coarse and fine.

how to make the block

Take your piece of untempered Masonite and rub it with the coarse sandpaper. This sanding will roughen the surface so the paint will adhere better. After sanding, cover the entire surface of the Masonite with water-base casein paint. Be sure the paint is creamy. Use a wide paint brush and long, continuous strokes in one direction. After one coat is finished, place the block near an open window to dry. It will not take long. When it is dry, apply a second coat, alternating the direction of the stroke. Let this coat dry. Apply five or six coats of paint in the same way, alternating the direction of the stroke with each layer and allowing each coat to dry thoroughly before applying the next.

The casein coating, when completed, should be at least 1/8″ thick. A thicker coating is better, if you are willing to take the time for preparation.

When the final coat is dry, the block is ready for smoothing out with fine sandpaper. Rub lightly, using long continuous strokes in one direction. Then dust with a soft cloth.

If you want a textured surface, skip the sanding. Instead, press metal mesh or coarse cloth such as burlap into the last layer of the paint while it is still moist. Remove, and let the paint dry. Or, for another variation of texture, you can sand some parts and not others.

When the block is thoroughly dry, it is ready for the next step. Now draw

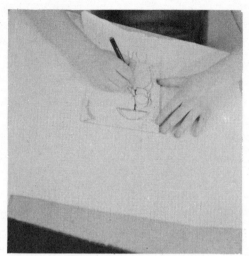

Drawing the design on the block with a crayon.

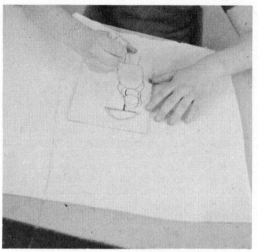

Squeezing a wet rag over the area to be cut in order to soften it.

your picture on it with a heavy crayon or a fountain brush. Use lines, rather than broad areas, for the casein block is particularly suitable for line work. You can even fill in the background with a line pattern—this is a shallow print and some of the background will print.

After the drawing is finished, the block is ready for cutting. Use a jig (page 12). Have at hand a bowl of water and several of the small cloths. Using one of the cloths, dampen the area of the block you are going to cut. Allow the water to soak in for a minute. Blot with a dry cloth. This soaking gives the casein the consistency of semi-hardened clay and makes it very easy to cut. Now you are ready to cut that part of the design which is on the softened area.

Follow the instructions on how to cut a block, in Chapter 1. You will find gougers and scoopers especially useful. After you have finished cutting the design into the softened area, prepare another area in the same way. Continue the soaking, blotting, and cutting procedure until the design is completely cut.

Set the block aside for 5 or 6 hours. Then it will be thoroughly dry and ready for printing.

how to print

The casein cut block is inked and printed in the same manner as most relief prints. Follow the general printing instructions in Chapter 1.

Cutting into the water-saturated surface.

Inking the block with an oil-base ink.

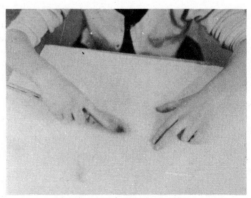

Printing with a spoon.

Pulling the print.

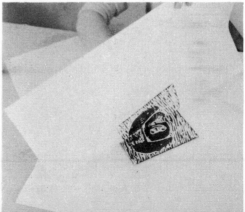

12
linocut print

The linocut, or linoleum print, is one of the commonest printmaking processes. In essence, it is a picture cut into a piece of linoleum and printed. People who like to design and print their own greeting cards most often use linoleum blocks. The quality of the linoleum and its lack of grain make it easier to work with than the woodcut, and it stands up equally well under printing.

The smooth linoleum surface produces pictures with very little texture and strong contrasts of solid black and pure white. Lines are bold and coarse. The linocut is a true relief cut. Any surface left in relief on the block will print. You can make white designs on a black background by gouging away the design, or black designs on a white background by gouging away the background. If you have had little or no experience with linocuts it is best to start with a design composed of large simple areas drawn on the block before cutting. As you become more and more skilled, you will find yourself depending less and less on the pre-drawing. Eventually you will prefer to cut directly into the linoleum without guiding lines. Such direct-cut prints have a certain dash and spontaneity hard to achieve by following specific lines with a knife.

The linocut requires coordination to control the tools. However, it is not a difficult process if you start slowly and proceed one step at a time. Very soon you will be able to produce prints that you will want to frame or send to your friends as greetings.

basic tools and materials

Wooden spoon

Cutting tools:
  The gougers and scoopers will be especially useful.

Crayon or fountain brush

Ink

Inking slab

Roller

Printing paper

Turpentine, newspapers, and rags

63

additional materials

Linoleum

Heavy "battleship" linoleum, mounted on blocks, can be bought in art stores. However, unmounted pieces, which are just as good, can usually be bought in floorcovering stores at considerable savings. In fact, many stores are glad to give away "end" or scrap pieces that are completely satisfactory for making linocut blocks.

how to make the block

The linoleum block needs no preparation. However, in cold weather the linoleum may be stiff. If it is, allow it to warm-up to room temperature before using in order to soften it and make cutting easier.

Draw a picture directly on the linoleum with a heavy crayon or a fountain brush. Remember that it is difficult to cut small intricate lines, so keep your drawing simple, use wide lines and large areas of black. When you are satisfied with your drawing, your block is ready to cut.

Cut the block according to the instructions in Chapter 1, and be sure to use the jig (page 12). You will find the gougers and scoopers especially useful for cutting the linoleum block.

After the cutting is completed, dust off the block and it is ready for printing.

how to print

The linocut is inked and printed in the same manner as most relief prints. Follow the general printing instructions in Chapter 1.

Drawing the design on the surface of the block.

Cutting the block which has been placed on a jig for protection.

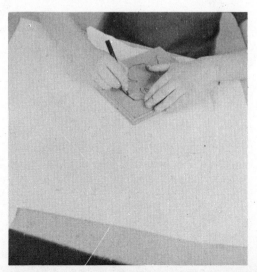

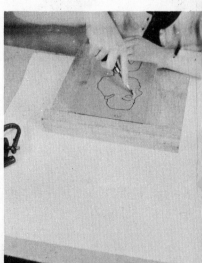

woodcut print

Although this old established process has long been used to produce prints of great distinction, producing them with a wooden spoon instead of a printing press is a new idea. By using the wooden spoon method described in this book, you can now make woodcut prints, from start to finish, right in your own home with the simplest of materials.

The method is similar to that of most cut relief prints; that is, areas not to print are cut away and the raised surface left on the block is printed. However, you have wood to contend with, and that is why the woodcut is the most difficult of all the relief processes and the most challenging. It requires care and patience for successful results. It is a mature means of expression and appeals to persons interested in developing skill in an established and well-recognized art medium.

Most of us are familiar with the appearance of a woodcut print. The grain of the wood is the predominant influence. It usually shows in the finished print, adding to the characteristic woodcut look. The grain direction is so strong that it affects the cutting in many ways. A cut made against the direction of the grain will be entirely different from one made with the grain, and will print differently. With practice you will learn to make use of the qualities of the wood to enrich your design.

While this is not a quick and easy process, a good woodcut is a real accomplishment and a source of great satisfaction. Interesting group work can be done by dividing a block into sections and having a different person work on each section, as was done in making this print.

Conclusion

basic tools and materials

Wooden spoon	Inking slab
Crayon or fountain brush	Roller
Cutting tools	Printing paper
Ink	Turpentine, newspapers, and rags

additional materials

Wood
Suitable wood can be bought at a lumber yard. Ask for clear pine or other soft wood, free of knots and with as little grain as possible. Tell the lumber dealer what the wood will be used for and ask him to cut it to the proper size.

Drawing the design on the surface of the block with a crayon.

Cutting the block. When making a woodcut block, always use a jig for protection.

Inking the block.

how to make the block

You must draw your design completely on the block before you start to cut. For drawing, use a heavy crayon or, even better, a fountain brush or other brush and ink. Until you are thoroughly experienced and confident, keep your picture very simple with large areas of black to reduce the amount of cutting. *Always use a jig* (page 12). This is essential when cutting a wood block, because of the grain and hardness of the material. Follow the cutting instructions in Chapter 1.

If you are entirely inexperienced in woodcutting, practice cutting methods on an odd piece of wood before you start the actual block. Your cutting knife will be your most useful tool. Always keep your free hand out of the path of the knife. Cut as deeply as possible, tracing the edges of all the black areas. Next, retrace these areas, cutting about $\frac{1}{16}''$ from the first cut and at an opposite angle. The result will be a V-shaped groove around the black areas. Everything that is not to print can now be scooped out with the U-shaped gouger. When all the areas that are not to print are cleared away, smooth out any remaining ridges with the chisel. Ease with the material, as well as appreciation of its possibilities, will come with experience.

Give your work a final check. Brush away all loose bits of wood. Then the block is ready for printing.

how to print

The woodcut is inked and printed in the same manner as most relief prints. Follow the printing instructions in Chapter 1.

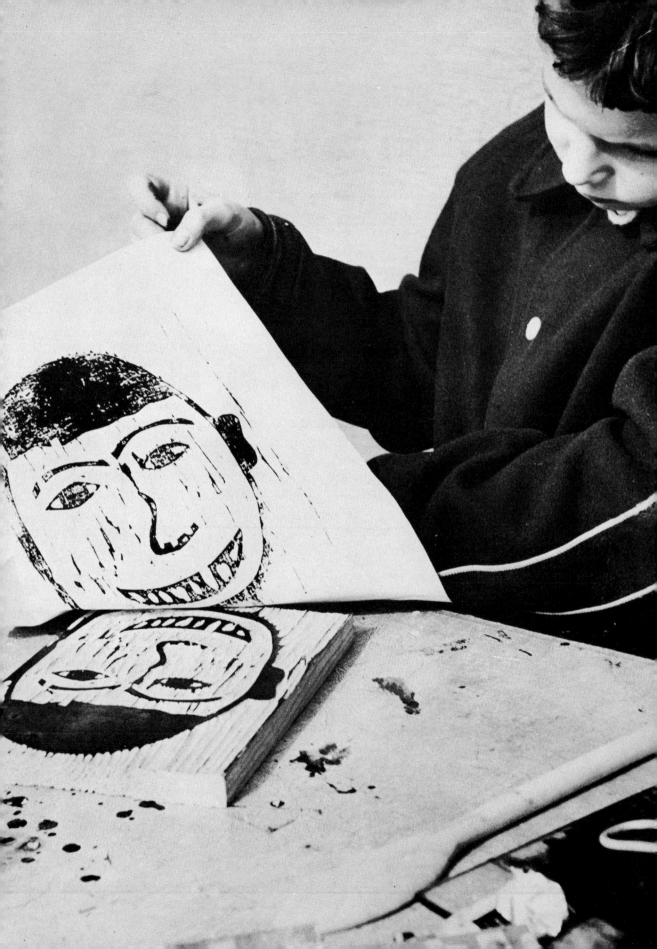

14

how to make pictures without printing

Here is a free-and-easy new way to work with print blocks. Skip the printing entirely and make relief block pictures instead of prints. The drip and cemented blocks (bean, string, cardboard) have this interesting extra possibility.

Block pictures are actually the finished relief block, before printing. To make a block picture simply follow the directions for making the print block, but do not ink it. It will not be printed; it is a picture in its own right.

Although the method is the same, you have much more freedom when you are making a block picture than you do with a block that will be used for printing, because you do not have to consider printing problems. You can give your imagination full play. You can try effects of every kind; for example, patterned cardboard backing, a backing of gold or silver paper pasted on cardboard. Each method offers its own opportunities for originality and experimentation. For the bean picture you can use beans of any shape, size, or color without a thought as to whether or not they will print well. The string picture can be gay with colored string, and varied by using thick, thin, knotted, even frayed string. The cardboard picture lends itself to mosaic treatment, or try a Joseph's coat of many colors. By using colored lacquers, the drip picture can glow with stained glass tones, sparkle with mosaic designs or multi-color stippel backgrounds. For a stark, modernistic look, try white lacquer on black cardboard.

You can combine the bean, string, cardboard, and drip picture methods in many ways to get effects of almost endless variety.

While block pictures are not graphic art, since they will not be reproduced, they are a good creative art medium nevertheless. Block pictures are a simple, new way for creative expression and experimentation. There is no difficult technique to discourage the imagination and results are immediate.

YOU CAN MOUNT OR FRAME YOUR PRINT BLOCK AFTER PRINTING, TOO.

After you have made as many prints as you want, use the block to make a decorative wall plaque. Its fun to have hanging on your wall the block from which you have made prints. To make a plaque, wipe off the print block, cover it with two coats of commercial flat white paint, let the paint dry, then roll black or colored ink over it. The same principle applies as in painting: only the relief areas will take ink and you will have a black or colored design against a white background. Instead or in addition to inking it with the roller, you can hand-color the block any way you choose. Mount or frame it and hang it up. All the print blocks can be used in this way, excepting the paper, potato, and mo-glu blocks.